Silly About Cats

Silly About Cats

THE BEST CAT CARTOONS FROM
AMERICAN AND BRITISH PERIODICALS

Edited by

Marbeth Reed

Doubleday & Company, Inc.
Garden City, New York

Acknowledgments

Permission to reprint the cartoons used in this book has been graciously given by the artists or their agents and the publications in which the drawings originally appeared.

Acknowledgment is made to the following:

Ajay, Anton, A. E. Beard, Janice and Stanley Berenstain, Bo Brown, Scott Brown, Dick Cavalli, Chaval, Paul Darrow, Walt Disney, Roland Fiddy, Stan Fine, F. Folkes, John Gallagher, Gantriis, Martin Giuffre, Herb Green, Larry Harris, Hoffnung, Al Johns, Maurice Jones, NIK, Hank Ketcham, Ted Key, Lamb, David Langdon, Lepper, Gustav Lundberg, Fred Lundy, Maurice McLoughlin, Harry Mace, Leslie Marchant, Jerry Marcus, Vic Martin, Ed Nofziger, Larry Reynolds, Cedric Rogers, Sebastian, Sonya Schus, Charles Sharman, Shirvanian, Siggs, Smilby, Ton Smits, Sprod, Starke, Henry Syverson, Jack Tippit, Don Tobin, Waite, Mort Walker, A. F. Wiles, Roy Wilson, Wimsey, B. Wiseman, and George Wolfe.

A. S. Knight, Ltd., The Ben Roth Agency, Hulton Press, Ltd., The Norman Agency, and Walt Disney Productions.

The American Legion Magazine, The American Magazine, Collier's, Everybody's, The Farm Journal, Liberty, Lilliput, The London Daily Sketch, MacLean's, The New York Times, Punch, The Saturday Evening Post, This Week, and Today's Health.

Avis

This is a study of various feline diversions made by some rather acute observers from here and abroad. Since it is based on real life situations, certain cats may consider it an invasion of privacy.

THE EDITOR

"I suppose they think that's funny."

"Get the license number!"

"What good will it be...it doesn't bark...
lay eggs...give milk..."

"Can't you get a job where the boss has a *tom* cat?"

"You forgot the cat food again."

"You must thank Philip for his lovely gift, Carol. Isn't that your father I see running down the street, Philip?"

"Stop stamping your feet!"

TON SMITS

18

"We leave them on doorsteps...it's practically doubled business."

"Either we get rid of her or buy drapes!"

21

HAZEL

"Eye dropper."

"They were most generous—insisted we take them all."

"Oh, for goodness' sake! Here she is!"

By Bo Brown. Copyright, 1957, by Bo Brown.

1.

2.

By Shirvanian. Copyright, 1953, by The Curtis Publishing Company.

24

"Should liven things up a bit—here comes a dog!"

"I suppose by rights we should be crying!"

"I'm sorry—they're not for sale"

1.

2.   3.   4.   5.

6.

"Certainly is nice of you to take the last of the kittens off our hands."

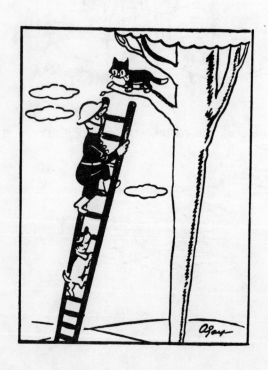

"I make her leave it as she found it."

"Isn't one pet in the family enough?"

"Melissa! I'll cut you out of my will!"

"Well, I hope you'll decide soon.
They're going like hot cakes."

"Well, first I'd want to inspect your home—
and then of course I'd need some sort of
reference."

"If you're such a good watchdog...what time is it?"

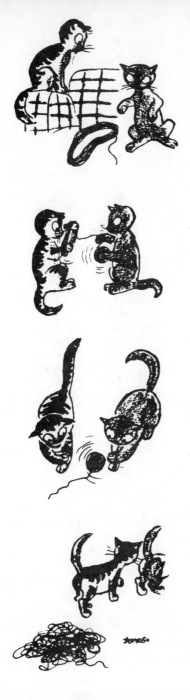

"She says she wants to come in and swing awhile!"

"Of course it makes a difference when you bring them up together."

By Ajay. Copyright, 1949, by Arthur Jackson.

"You may make ivory, but you haven't got what it takes to make violin strings!"

"But I don't encourage them—I just give them something to eat."

"I'm a grandmother!"

BUTCH

"Yeah, I plan to visit a coupla other houses tonight. Why?"

SYVERSON

47

48

"Guess who's going to be a mother."

"Now!"

55

"Not only did I fail to give any away, but when I stopped in at the drugstore for a minute, somebody sneaked *three more in*."

"I'm afraid you're in her chair."

"Found her."

"Then I asked Sarah Jane's mommy if I could have one of Queenie's kittens and Sarah Jane's daddy said..."

"If darling Tibby so much as sniffs at my budgies
I'll knock his darling block off."

SISTER

"That nice Mrs. Dugan is moving into some mean old apartment house that doesn't allow pets."

SYVERSON

"It says: 'Hello, Daddy — Mom sent us over to live with you!'"

"She was a poor investment—she eats more than the mice did!"

"Comfy?"

1

2

4

1.

2.

5.

3.

4.

6.

7.

jack
o a
tippit

"Oh nonsense! The mouse enjoys it as much as pussy."

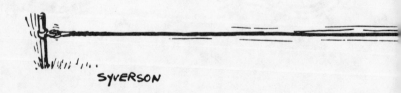

"The man was darn' nice! He invited all of us boys in, gave each one of us a bottle of pop and a kitten, and never even mentioned his broken window."

"Don't walk in front of me!"

"Interesting little break in routine this, Wilkinson."

"We're running low on friends."

"Now that we're all here we'll proceed with the reading of your Aunt Matilda's will!"

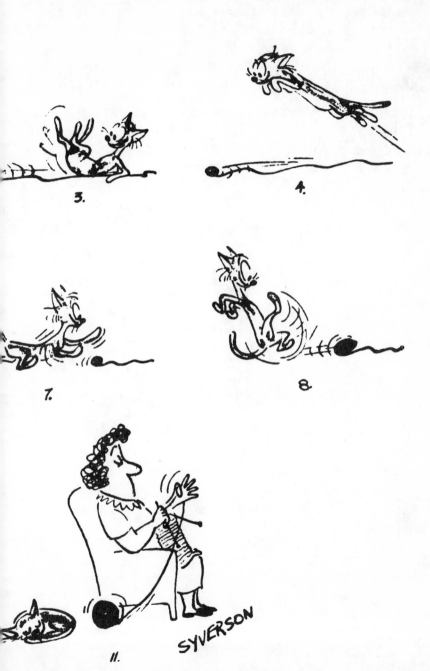

3.

4.

7.

8.

SYVERSON

11.

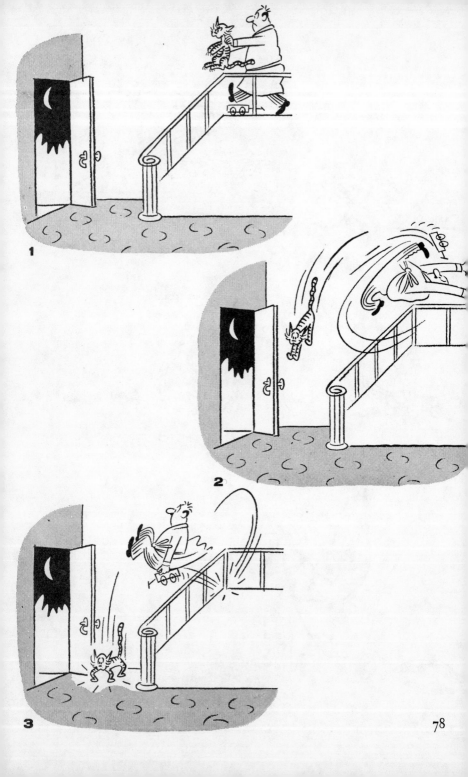

1.

2.

3.

4.

5.

6.

7.

8.

9.

10.   SYVERSON

81

"We always keep one out of a litter."

"Do you realize we haven't one real friend in this town!"

"Here, kitty, kitty, kitty…"

"Hey! Your Majesty!"

"I thought I'd better ask. Some people don't like cats."

91

"It's all a matter of taste, but there're writers I've liked better."

93

"It's closing time—so relax the majestic pose, buddy!"